LEOPARDS

LIVING WILD

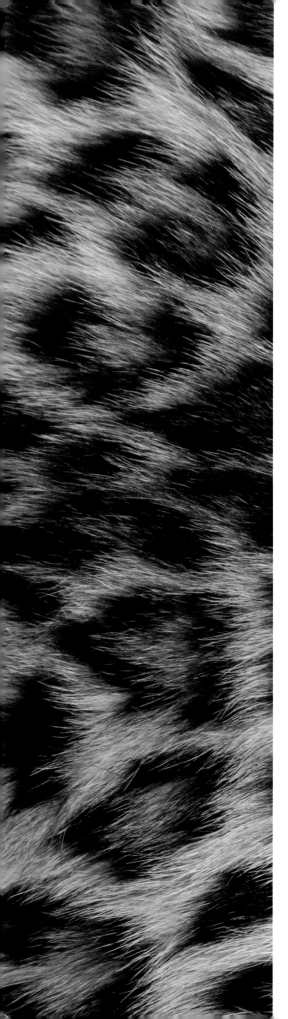

LIVING WILD

Published by Creative Education
P.O. Box 227, Mankato, Minnesota 56002
Creative Education is an imprint of The Creative Company
www.thecreativecompany.us

Design and production by Mary Herrmann
Art direction by Rita Marshall
Printed by Corporate Graphics in the United States of America

Photographs by 123RF (Keith Levit, Mahantesh C Morabad), Alamy (Paul Brough, The London Art Archive, Steve Bloom Images), Corbis (Nigel J. Dennis/Gallo Images, Bagla Pallava/Corbis Sygma), Dreamstime (Senai Aksoy, Kitchner Bain, Ewan Chesser, Arindom Chowdhury, Eric Gevaert, Darren Green, Igor Groshev, Hilton123, Konstantin Kirillov, Stephen Meese, Palko72, Johan Reineke, Mike Rogal), Getty Images (AFP, John Dominis, Art Wolfe, Kim Wolhuter), iStockphoto (Ewan Chesser, Jonathan Heger, Eric Hull, Benjamin Jessop, Gail A Johnson, Peter Malsbury, Tatiana Morozova, Graeme Prudy, Kristian Sekulic, Dieter Spears, Wolfgang Steiner, Peter Ten Broecke). Image on p. 32 from the collection of Gary Schulze, New York City. Used with permission.

Library of Congress Cataloging-in-Publication Data
Gish, Melissa.
Leopards / by Melissa Gish.
p. cm. — (Living wild)
Includes bibliographical references and index.
Summary: A look at leopards, including their habitats, physical characteristics such as their spotted fur, behaviors, relationships with humans, and threatened status in the world today.
ISBN 978-1-58341-972-4
1. Leopard—Juvenile literature. I. Title. II. Series.

QL737.C23G517 2010
599.75'54—dc22   2009025173

CPSIA: 120109 PO1092
First Edition
9 8 7 6 5 4 3 2 1

c CREATIVE EDUCATION

LEOPARDS

Melissa Gish

Night has fallen in South Africa's Kruger National Park. Hyenas yip in the distance as a

female leopard emerges from the tall,
dry grass beneath a baobab tree.

N ight has fallen in South Africa's Kruger National Park. Hyenas yip in the distance as a female leopard emerges from the tall, dry grass beneath a baobab tree. She crouches low and steps lightly, slowly advancing toward a herd of small Thomson's gazelles. Suddenly, she leaps forward and lands on the back of a young gazelle, slamming it to the ground and shattering its neck bones. Her jaws clamp onto the gazelle's throat, cutting off

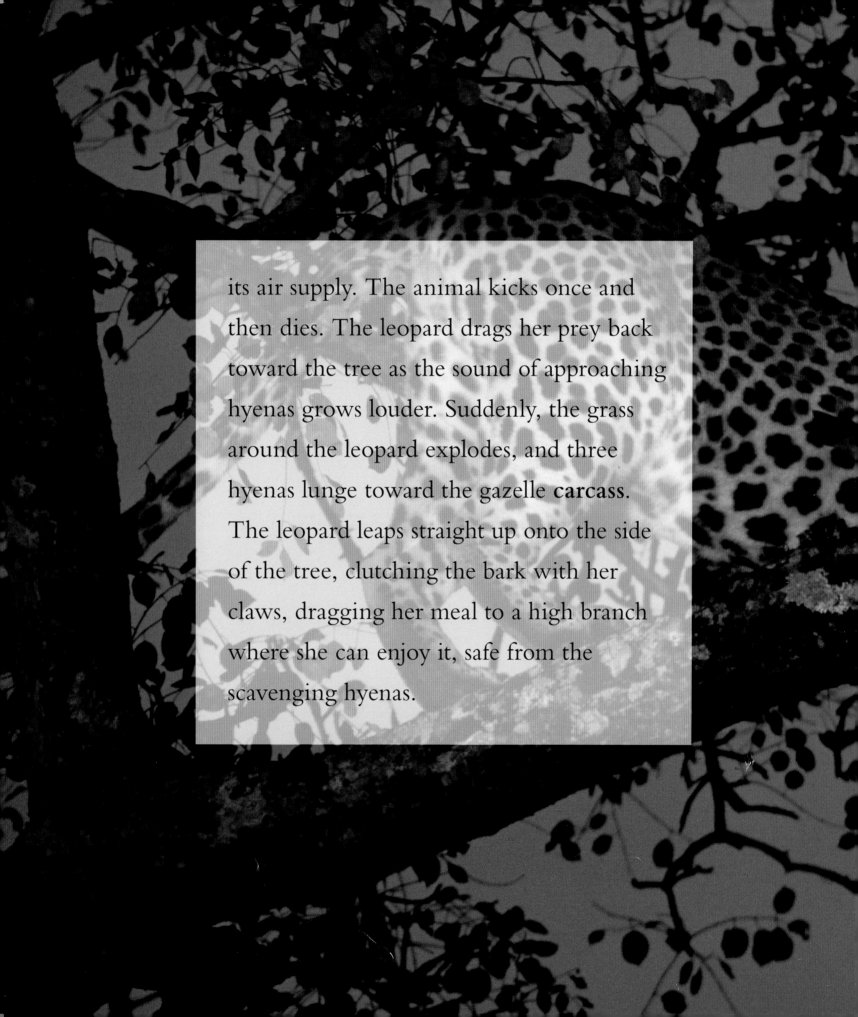

its air supply. The animal kicks once and then dies. The leopard drags her prey back toward the tree as the sound of approaching hyenas grows louder. Suddenly, the grass around the leopard explodes, and three hyenas lunge toward the gazelle **carcass**. The leopard leaps straight up onto the side of the tree, clutching the bark with her claws, dragging her meal to a high branch where she can enjoy it, safe from the scavenging hyenas.

WHERE IN THE WORLD THEY LIVE

■ **Amur Leopard**
southeastern
Russia, northern
China

□ **Arabian Leopard**
Saudi Arabia

■ **Sri Lankan
Leopard**
Sri Lanka

**Melanistic
Leopard**
Asian rainforests

■ **Javan Leopard**
Java, Indonesia

■ **African Leopard**
Africa south of the
Sahara Desert

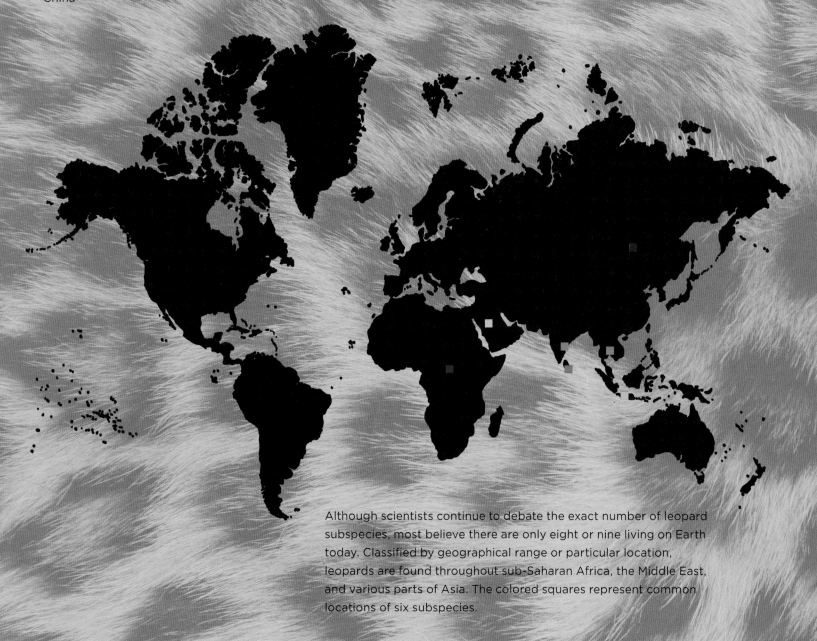

Although scientists continue to debate the exact number of leopard
subspecies, most believe there are only eight or nine living on Earth
today. Classified by geographical range or particular location,
leopards are found throughout sub-Saharan Africa, the Middle East,
and various parts of Asia. The colored squares represent common
locations of six subspecies.

SEEING SPOTS

The leopard is the smallest of the world's four species of big cats. Its closest relatives are the lion of Africa and India, the tiger of Asia, and the jaguar of Central and South America. Because they are highly **adaptable**, leopards are the most widespread of all large predators. They can survive in swampy rainforests as well as on rugged mountainsides. They are found in virtually every type of forest, grassland, and **semidesert** in India, central Asia, China, the Middle East, and sub-Saharan and northeastern Africa.

The big cats are members of the Felidae family and the genus *Panthera*, which is a group generally characterized as cats that roar. All cats typically growl, screech, and scream, but lions, tigers, jaguars, and leopards all roar. The leopard's roar sounds more like a loud cough, though. Leopards cough loudly to see if any other leopards are around. If there are, they will cough back.

The leopard's scientific name is *Panthera pardus*. The word "leopard" comes from the Greek word *leopardos*, which is a combination of the words *leon* (lion) and *pardos* (panther). The word "panther" is used to describe

African legend has it that the leopard's long whiskers possess magical powers.

Cheung-Chi, a North China leopard born in the Toronto Zoo in 1976, currently has more than 40 descendants in zoos around the world.

Other names for the Amur leopard include Far East, Manchurian, and Korean leopard.

The Amur leopard has the longest legs of any leopard, and its coat changes color from reddish gold in summer to pale cream during winter.

various big cats in different parts of the world. Cougars and jaguars, native to the Americas, are sometimes called panthers, as are African and Asian leopards.

There were once thought to be nearly 30 subspecies of leopard, each defined by its geographical location. For example, the Javan leopard is found only on the Indonesian island of Java, and the North China leopard is found only in northern China. To simplify matters, biologists are debating whether to combine various subspecies that have virtually identical **genetic** makeup and reclassify leopards into just eight or nine subspecies.

The Amur leopard of southeastern Russia and northern China is one of the rarest cats in the world. While nearly 300 Amur leopards live in zoos, fewer than 40 individuals survive in the wild—and only a handful are female. The Zanzibar leopard, native to Unguja Island (also called Zanzibar) off the east coast of Africa, may already be **extinct**. Researchers have not documented a sighting of a Zanzibar leopard since the early 1980s. Like many animals with beautiful fur, leopards have been relentlessly hunted for sport and profit since the mid-1800s.

Leopards are muscular animals with short, powerful legs

The Amur leopard's coat grows in length from one inch (2.5 cm) in summer to three inches (7.6 cm) in winter.

Unlike true leopards, which roar, the snow leopard's vocalizations include yowls, moans, and grunts.

and broad, rounded feet. Male leopards can weigh up to 180 pounds (82 kg). Females are smaller, usually about 120 pounds (54 kg). Leopards stand about 30 inches (76 cm) at the shoulder and can grow to be 6 feet (1.8 m) long. The tail may add an additional two to three feet (.6-.9 m).

Lions may grow to weigh 550 pounds (249 kg), and tigers can reach 650 pounds (295 kg). Because leopards are considerably smaller than lions and tigers, they tend to avoid areas inhabited by these cats. When a conflict between a leopard and a larger relative does occur, though, a leopard will almost always run, even if it means abandoning its food. Leopards may end up as prey because they are unable to outrun or to defend themselves against larger, hungrier cats.

The leopard has a number of relatives in the Felidae family, including the elusive clouded leopard of Southeast Asia and southern China; the snow leopard, which lives in the mountains of central Asia; and the cougar, which is native to the Americas. In addition to lions and tigers, another relative that may conflict with the leopard is the African cheetah. This cat is smaller than the leopard, but it is much faster and will sometimes snatch young leopards from their mothers.

The large, dark-edged, irregularly shaped spots of the clouded leopard are said to resemble clouds.

A male leopard regularly patrols its territory, following the same path and marking the same areas throughout its lifetime.

At first glance, a golden-colored leopard may be mistaken for a jaguar or a cheetah. But the spots actually differentiate between the species. Jaguars have black rosettes—dark, ring-like markings that are shaped like rose blossoms—with lines and spots inside them, and cheetahs have solid black spots. The leopard's rosettes are black with brown or golden centers. No two leopards

have the same markings. Like human fingerprints, each leopard's rosettes are unique.

The leopard's coloration also provides **camouflage**. In desert habitats such as southern Africa's vast Kalahari, leopard fur is light yellow like the surrounding sand. In grasslands and forested environments, such as in South Africa's MalaMala Game Reserve, leopards are a dark

While leopards and wildebeest can both run up to 36 miles (58 km) per hour, leopards can accelerate faster than their prey.

Leopards have a wider natural range around the world than almost all mammals except humans and wolves.

golden color that blends in with rocks and tree bark. The golden centers of a leopard's rosettes resemble the flashes of light that occur as sunlight penetrates the rainforests and grasses of the leopard's habitat. At night, the rosettes blend into the moonlit darkness.

Big cats known as black panthers are not really panthers but are melanistic—black-colored—leopards or jaguars. Melanism is an inherited trait that can occur in all cats but is most common in leopards or jaguars. Some scientists believe the trait is related to an animal's habitat. Melanistic leopards rarely occur in desert or grassland environments, where a darker coloration would not be a helpful camouflage, but they are common in about 50 percent of the populations found in the dense rainforests of Asia.

Although they appear to be completely black, melanistic leopards have rosettes just like other leopards. In certain lighting conditions, the markings become visible. However, in their thick forest habitat, these leopards become practically invisible, making them deadly hunters.

Leopards are nocturnal animals, which means that they are more active at night than during the day. Long whiskers and long eyebrow hairs protect the leopard's eyes

and help the cat feel its way through grass and bushes at night. Like many nocturnal animals, leopards have good night vision and are able to see in near darkness.

The leopard's eyes are equipped with a reflective layer of tissue called a tapetum lucidum. This tissue collects light and concentrates it in the center of the **retina**, allowing the leopard to see six times better than humans can in very low light. The tapetum lucidum causes eyeshine, a condition in which an animal's eyes reflect color when a light source is shined on them. The leopard's eyeshine is bright green in color.

Melanistic leopards and jaguars have an abundance of the chemical melanin, which causes dark-colored cells to form in hair and skin.

Leopards are the largest of all cat species that can count climbing trees among their regular habits.

SILENT HUNTERS

Leopards target more than 90 prey animals in Africa alone, including young giraffes.

Hiding in caves, rock crevices, tall grass, and trees to avoid predators such as larger leopards and lions, leopards sleep during the day—anywhere from 12 to 20 hours—and hunt very early in the morning or at night. They are not fussy eaters. Rather, they are opportunistic feeders, meaning they will eat any kind of prey that happens to be nearby—including the leftovers from a lion feast.

Leopards regularly hunt a wide range of prey that varies by geographic region. In Africa, leopards hunt baboons, Cape buffalo, Thomson's gazelles, and wildebeest—targeting the young, old, and ill. In China and other parts of Asia, Chinese water deer and monkeys are hunted, and in desert regions, leopards eat anything from birds and rodents to grasshoppers. Regardless of a leopard's habitat, nothing is too small to provide a snack.

Unlike the cheetah, a cat built for short bursts of speed as it chases its prey, the leopard is built for launching surprise attacks. Although they are capable of sprinting at speeds of up to 36 miles (58 km) per hour, leopards choose to sneak up on prey instead. Thick pads on the

The Somali leopard of Somalia and Ethiopia is the smallest of all leopards, with males weighing only 50 to 60 pounds (22.6 to 27.2 kg).

Although doglike in appearance, hyenas belong to Feliformia, the suborder of catlike carnivores.

The Indian leopard has many predators—such as Asiatic lions, tigers, bears, hyenas, and wild dogs—all of which frequently kill leopard cubs.

bottoms of their feet provide a cushion as they creep silently toward prey before pouncing, and then they can jump forward 20 feet (6 m). To kill prey, the leopard's powerful jaws pierce the prey's throat, cutting off its air supply, while the leopard's long, **retractable** claws dig into the animal to hold it still until it suffocates.

Leopards must remain ever watchful for predators as well as sneaky competitors such as baboons and hyenas. These animals regularly steal leopard kills. To avoid being robbed of its meal, a leopard will hide its food in a deep cave or stash it in a tree. Research has revealed that the leopard can leap 10 feet (3 m) off the ground to clamp its claws into tree bark while carrying up to 60 pounds (27 kg) of dead weight in its mouth.

The leopard is a solitary animal, living alone in a particular area called its home range. The size of a home range varies from as small as 12 square miles (31 sq km) to as large as approximately 116 square miles (300 sq km), depending on how many leopards exist in a region. A leopard marks the boundaries of its home range by spraying urine and making deep scratches on trees. It will also roar to announce its presence to other leopards.

Leopards first tear out patches of fur from prey and then eat from the cleaned-off part, saving the rest for later.

Leopards typically mate with several partners found in neighboring or overlapping home ranges.

Because female leopards' home ranges overlap anyway, they will return to the site where they were born to give birth to their own young.

Males travel all around their territory, marking the boundaries over and over. They rarely stay in one spot for more than a few days. Females, on the other hand, travel little and scent-mark their boundaries only occasionally, instead making coughing sounds to keep intruders away. Home ranges may overlap, but leopards tend to stay out of each other's way. Even if a male allows a number of females to establish their own individual home ranges within his larger home range, he will not have contact with them except during mating season.

When a female is ready to mate, male leopards are drawn to her by a certain smell that is released in her urine markings. Leopards mate year round in most places, but in the cold areas of northern China and Siberia, mating season occurs only in January and February. A male and female will come together for up to six days, mating many times to ensure success. Then the male will leave the female.

Before she gives birth, the female leopard selects several den sites—in tree cavities, thick brush, or caves—where she and her offspring will be safe from predators. After 90 to 105 days, the female gives birth. Leopards usually

have two or three cubs, but up to six may be born in rare instances. The mother will move her young from place to place in order to protect them from lions, hyenas, crocodiles, and other large meat-eaters that often make meals of young leopards. The **mortality rate** of cubs is high. If a mother leopard manages to keep one cub alive through maturity—about two years—she is lucky.

Cubs weigh only about 1.2 pounds (544 g) at birth. When cubs are born, the spots on their coats are very close together, making their fur appear a solid grayish brown. They have blue eyes that do not open until the

Cubs are born blind but soon learn to hunt, pouncing on grasshoppers, frogs, mice, and small birds.

Leopards can detect sounds up to a mile (1.6 km) away, making a sighting of them rare, even on a reserve.

cubs are 10 days old. As cubs grow, their eyes will darken to a golden brown, and the rosettes on their coats will spread out.

Cubs rely on their mother's milk for nourishment for the first three to four months of their lives, but as soon as six weeks after birth, their mother will introduce them to meat. The cubs remain hidden in tall grass or crouched in a tree until their mother has captured prey. Then the

cubs will follow their mother up a tree to share the meal. When the cubs are about four months old, they will begin to join their mother on hunts.

By the time they are one year of age, leopard cubs can fend for themselves, yet they remain with their mothers for another year or more. It takes time for young leopards to fine-tune their hunting skills, so they continue to hunt with their mother, sharing kills with her, until they are 24 to 30 months old.

By this time, the young leopards are fully mature, and their mother will chase them away. The young leopards go off alone in search of territories that have not yet been claimed or that have been abandoned by leopards that have died or moved away. A female cub may be allowed to take a portion of her mother's home range and make it her own, but males must move away so they will not be in competition with older males in the area.

Because leopards are difficult to monitor, it is not known for certain how long these elusive cats can live in the wild. Some studies suggest that leopards survive no more than 10 to 15 years. But in captivity, leopards may live more than 20 years.

When resting, a snow leopard wraps its long, thick tail around its body and face as protection against the cold.

Leopard fur has traditionally been associated with royalty, as evidenced in Egyptian artwork dating from 2590 B.C.

STEALTH AND SPIRIT

T hroughout human history, leopards have symbolized power, fearlessness, and intelligence. Unlike lions or tigers, which utilize brute strength, the leopard is a cunning predator that exemplifies how success is not measured by physical size alone. Leopards are also beautiful creatures that express grace and elegance.

Osiris, one of the most powerful gods in Egyptian **mythology**, was often pictured wearing a leopard skin. As a god of fertility, Osiris was associated with creative energy and success in agriculture. People in ancient Egypt would wear a leopard tail on a belt or around the neck as a charm that provided strength and protection from misfortune.

Ancient Greek mythology transformed Osiris into the Greek god Dionysus, who wore leopard skins and rode on a leopard's back or in a chariot pulled by leopards. Dionysus was a god of fruitfulness and vegetation but was especially known as a god of wine and celebration. Followers of Dionysus lived their lives joyously and without fear. Several famous 2,000-year-old Greek **mosaics** show Dionysus riding a leopard.

Romans in the second century A.D. took the ancient Greek art of mosaics to a newly intricate and more colorful level.

The former French colony of Middle Congo (Moyen-Congo) featured ivory tusks and leopards on its postage.

The leopard appears on many countries' flags and official seals, such as on the coat of arms of the Democratic Republic of the Congo.

Throughout the ancient Arab and Mesopotamian world (which covered the present-day lands of the Middle East), stories arose of a mighty hunter named Nimrod (also known as Hoshang), a Babylonian king associated with the biblical story of the Tower of Babel. According to legend, "Nimrod" was derived from his Persian name, Nimr Raad, which means "leopard tamer," because he sometimes used a leopard in place of a hunting dog and often wore leopard skins.

About 5,000 years ago, the people of Mesopotamia created a huge mural showing red and black leopards standing guard over the entrance to a holy place. And in China, leopards were carved in ancient stone as symbols of fearless protection. An even older example of leopards in ancient culture appears in the remains of a village in southern Turkey, Çatalhöyük, where an 8,000-year-old **shrine** dedicated to leopards was **excavated** between 1961 and 1965. The walls are covered with sculptures and murals that include human-like figures riding leopards, holding leopard cubs, and sitting on leopard thrones. Historians believe that leopards were important spirits in the ancient peoples' culture.

THE OUTSONG: BAGHEERA

In the cage my life began;
Well I know the worth of Man.
By the Broken Lock that freed—
Man-cub, 'ware the Man-cub's breed!
Scenting-dew or starlight pale,
Choose no tangled tree-cat trail.
Pack or council, hunt or den,
Cry no truce with Jackal-Men.
Feed them silence when they say:
"Come with us an easy way."
Feed them silence when they seek
Help of thine to hurt the weak.

Make no bandar's boast of skill;
Hold thy peace above the kill.
Let nor call nor song nor sign
Turn thee from thy hunting-line.
(Morning mist or twilight clear,
Serve him, Wardens of the Deer!)

Wood and Water, Wind and Tree,
Jungle-Favour go with thee!

Rudyard Kipling (1865–1936),
from The Jungle Book

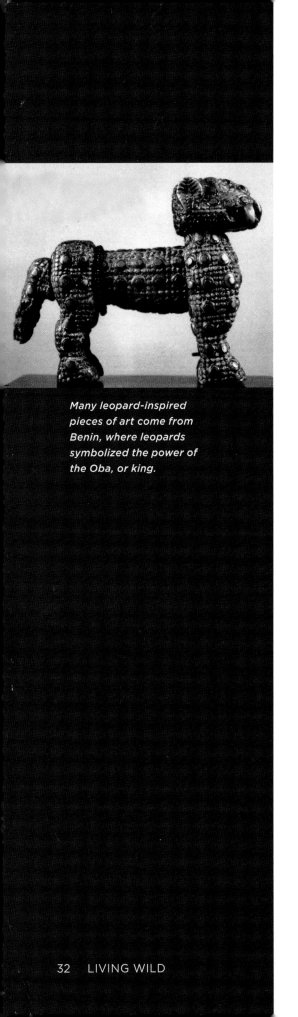

Many leopard-inspired pieces of art come from Benin, where leopards symbolized the power of the Oba, or king.

Throughout Africa, early cultures saw the leopard as a totem animal, or good luck charm. People even carved miniature statues of leopards and carried them around. Historians highly value two particular artifacts from the former West African country of Benin (now a city in the country of Nigeria): leopards carved from ivory whose spots are made with European bullets. These leopards, seized by the British military when it invaded Benin in 1897, were given to England's Queen Victoria. They are now on display at the British Museum in London.

The leopard continues to be an important part of African cultural rituals and customs in modern times. Tribes in Nigeria and Cameroon still sometimes practice a custom called leopard-giving. When a hunter kills a leopard, the animal is given to the village chief, who thanks the animal for giving its life for his village before butchering it and sharing the meat with village leaders. These men are known as "the leopard people," and they believe that consuming the meat of the leopard gives them strength and good judgment to continue leading their village.

Leopards are also feared and hated by some humans. For as long as humans and leopards have shared habitats,

there have been deadly encounters. Because they are so stealthy, leopards can venture into human-populated areas undetected. They will attack livestock and even domestic dogs—and when desperate for food or feeling defensive, they sometimes even go after humans.

Leopards that have attacked humans are labeled "man-eaters" and considered dangerous. Game wardens and other officials will hunt down man-eating leopards and will either destroy or trap and relocate them. Many farmers take matters into their own hands and poison or shoot leopards that threaten their livestock.

Poaching also poses a major threat to leopards, especially in India and Asia. Tiger **pelts**, bones, and organs are highly prized around the world, and, despite having been on the Endangered Species List since 1969, tigers are now critically endangered and facing extinction (largely due to poaching). Because of this, animal traders have turned their attention to leopards, illegally killing them for their pelts, which are made into coats and rugs, and their teeth, claws, bones, and organs—all of which serve some purpose to collectors and those who practice traditional folk medicine.

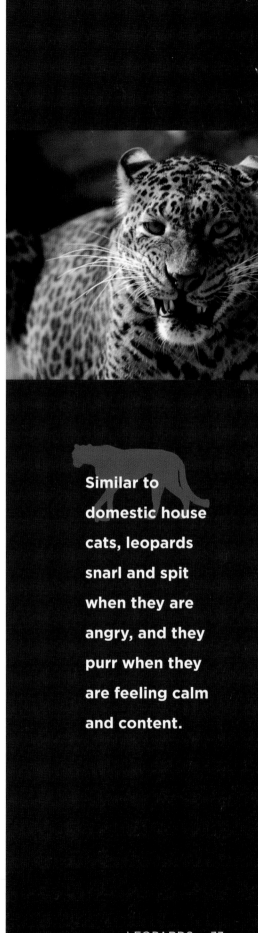

Similar to domestic house cats, leopards snarl and spit when they are angry, and they purr when they are feeling calm and content.

The goatlike Nilgiri tahr (above) and its Arabian relative are endangered due to overhunting.

Fewer than 250 Arabian leopards exist in Middle Eastern mountains, where their major prey—mountain gazelles and tahrs—are also nearly extinct.

In Africa, the leopard population is likely in the millions, but in Asia, only about 18,000 leopards exist—with 80 percent of them living in India. In many parts of the world, such as Syria and Lebanon, leopards have been hunted to total extinction. Yet in other places, such as the Indian city of Mysore, a healthy leopard population exists side-by-side with people. Unless a leopard wanders into the city by mistake, residents usually leave the animals alone.

In literature, leopards are sometimes portrayed as thoughtful animals. In 1830, French author Honoré de Balzac wrote "A Passion in the Desert," a story about a soldier lost in the Egyptian desert who is befriended by a leopard. The two form a unique bond when, instead of attacking the soldier, the leopard shows him where to find water and shares her food with him.

Perhaps the best-loved leopard in literature is Bagheera, a black panther (or melanistic leopard), who befriends the boy Mowgli in Rudyard Kipling's *The Jungle Book* (1894) and *The Second Jungle Book* (1895). Bagheera becomes Mowgli's caretaker and helps him outsmart the hungry tiger Shere Khan. Kipling also wrote a series of fantastical stories that explained how certain things came to be. His

book of *Just So Stories* (1902) included the tale "How the Leopard Got His Spots."

Additionally, in Edgar Rice Burroughs's famous book *Tarzan of the Apes* (1914), a gorilla is responsible for orphaning young Tarzan, but in the 1999 Walt Disney film version, *Tarzan*, it is a leopard that kills Tarzan's human parents. Tarzan later takes over as leader of his gorilla family when he kills the leopard and presents it to his gorilla father in a leopard-giving ritual.

Leopards have a reputation for being aimless killers, but they attack humans only out of desperation or self-defense.

Researchers may weigh a leopard and test its blood before fitting the big cat with a trackable collar.

KEEPING THEIR SECRETS

As human populations continue to expand into wilderness areas, leopards are forced into having more contact with people, which often leads to conflict and the destruction of leopards. Researchers also believe that up to 1,500 people die each year from being attacked by big cats (lions, tigers, jaguars, and leopards). As scientists discover more about leopard origins and behaviors, they are also working to find ways of keeping leopards and humans safe from one another.

According to fossil records, the first cats emerged about 25 million years ago. These included three groups: large cats, small cats, and saber-toothed cats (including the well-known genus *Smilodon*). Most of these early species eventually died out. Scientists believe that modern cats share one common ancestor that existed in Asia nearly 11 million years ago. As this prehistoric cat spread across Asia, Africa, northern Europe, and over the Bering **Land Bridge** between Siberia and Alaska, it began to **evolve** into separate species that adapted to the various climates, landscapes, and food sources of their respective habitats.

Leopards keep their claws—which are made of a hard substance called keratin—healthy and sharp by scratching tree bark.

The first leopards, which appeared about 3.8 million years ago, resembled jaguars but had shorter limbs and bigger, heavier bodies. Some of the oldest fossils of these leopards have been found in the African country of Tanzania. True leopards appeared in Africa between 500,000 and 800,000 years ago and then moved across Asia 200,000 to 300,000 years ago. Fossils of the first modern leopards have been found from southern Asia to Africa and throughout Europe. These leopards eventually died out everywhere but in Asia and Africa.

Scientists found that early leopards, in addition to climbing trees, used caves to store their food. This would have prevented competitors, such as hyenas, from stealing the food because they could not see as well in the dark as leopards. In addition to hunting hoofed animals, birds, and apes, the first leopards preyed on early humans. A 1948 study of a South African cave revealed a two-million-year-old hominid (human) skull bearing two puncture marks, each the size of a dime and matching the spacing of a leopard's long front teeth. The leopard probably would have dragged this person into a tree for a meal.

Despite worldwide attention to declining populations of big cats, demand still exists for illegal tiger and leopard pelts.

Since 2002, conservation efforts in India have helped leopard and sloth bear (above) populations rebound. ›

The earliest humans did not regularly hunt leopards for food, but they undoubtedly killed leopards in self-defense. Later, as humans developed more powerful weapons, such as sharp spears, they targeted leopards for their fur, which became a status symbol of power and was worn by tribal chiefs. Hunting—both by natives and eventually by Europeans—continued over many generations, until leopards began to disappear from many of their original habitats.

In Africa, numerous game reserves and national parks protect leopards from hunters, which has enabled leopard populations in many parts of Africa to stabilize and grow healthy. In Asia, however, leopards are at risk of extinction, despite living in similar game reserves and parks. Poachers trespass illegally, and when leopards wander outside the borders of protected areas, they are often killed.

To raise funds to help cover management costs, many parks allow visitors to track leopards—with cameras instead of guns—for a fee. Several national parks on the Asian island of Sri Lanka are home to the world's remaining 600 Sri Lankan leopards. These parks welcome people to view the leopards—as well as other protected species such as elephants and sloth bears—on guided jeep

tours. The leopards have become accustomed to the jeeps and regularly approach the vehicles so visitors can take close-up photographs.

Programs to help save endangered leopards have been underway for the past 30 years. The Amur leopard, admired for its particularly thick coat, has been hunted to near extinction. **Captive-rearing** programs in America and Europe are designed to help the Amur leopard repopulate so that the young can be released into the wilds of their native China and Russia. These programs have not been highly successful, though, and scientists fear the Amur leopard could be extinct by 2020.

The best hope endangered leopards have for survival is if the people who share their environment become more educated about them. In the African nation of Botswana, leopards are endangered because of habitat loss. As agriculture and ranching expand, farmers who see leopards as threats to their livestock frequently kill the big cats. One of the goals of the Leopard Ecology & Conservation project in Botswana's Khutse Game Reserve is to develop successful methods of protecting livestock from leopards, thus reducing the number of leopard deaths.

Leopards can survive up to a month without drinking water, getting moisture from the tissues and organs of the animals they eat.

The native San people of southern Africa consider the leopard the most deadly hunter, calling it "silent killer."

No leopards have ever existed in Australia, yet Monash University in Melbourne, Australia, is highly concerned about the future of leopards in South Africa, where the school has a branch campus in the city of Johannesburg. Its MunYaWana Leopard Project is the first to study leopards in the KwaZulu-Natal region of South Africa. It compares populations of leopards living inside protected areas with populations residing outside. By studying the feeding and mating patterns of the two groups of leopards, the project hopes to establish a management plan that will eventually protect leopards outside reserves.

Because leopards are difficult to track and capture, research on individuals is not easily accomplished. Namibia's Erindi Private Game Reserve conducts research on its resident leopards by trapping them and temporarily fitting them with **radio collars**. Flying overhead in a small airplane, researchers can track the movements of the leopards, and traveling by jeep or on foot into the leopards' territories offers an up-close view of their behaviors. Since the project began in 2007, five leopards have been collared. The research will offer insights into how leopards select and patrol their home ranges.

The leopard is one of the world's biggest and most beautiful cats. As a large predator, it is vital to the health of its habitats' **food chains** in Africa and Asia. Researchers have only begun to uncover the mysteries of this elusive animal, yet surely these amazing cats have more secrets to reveal, if only their unstable populations can survive human persecution long enough.

Like other cats, leopards spend about two-thirds of their lives resting or sleeping, usually in the safety of trees.

ANIMAL TALE: WHY LEOPARDS AND BABOONS ARE ENEMIES

The relationship between leopards and baboons is not a friendly one. Leopards make meals of baboons, while baboons routinely steal meals from leopards. This folktale from the Zulu, the largest **ethnic** group in South Africa, reveals the origins behind the unfriendly behavior exhibited by each animal toward the other.

Long ago, Leopard and Baboon shared the land in peace. They met here and there, politely nodding to one another as they passed. Early one morning, before the sun had crept far above the horizon, Leopard began chasing Dassie, the rock hyrax, who scuttled along looking like a large guinea pig.

As Leopard chased her, Dassie darted toward a huge anthill and disappeared down its hole. Leopard reached her paw down the hole, but it was too deep, and she could not reach Dassie. For a long time, Leopard scratched at the anthill, but she still could not reach Dassie. As the sun rose higher in the sky, Leopard began to feel hot.

Just then, Baboon passed by. "You look very hot," Baboon said to Leopard. "You should go to the river and take a swim and have a drink of water."

"I do not want to leave," Leopard said. "I am very hungry and must wait for Dassie to emerge from this hole."

"I will stand guard," Baboon said. "You go to the river, and when Dassie emerges, I will grab her and hold her for you."

"Thank you, friend," Leopard said as she ran down the hill toward the river.

Baboon settled down against the anthill, happy to sun himself on the warm sand. Soon, he fell asleep and began snoring. Dassie, hearing Baboon's snoring, crept

out of the hole. Leopard returned to the anthill just in time to see Dassie disappear into the tall grass.

Leopard angrily pounced on Baboon and slapped him awake. "You worthless ape!" she roared, insulting him greatly by calling him an ape, for baboons are not apes. "My breakfast just ran down the hill!"

Leopard's anger frightened Baboon, and he started to back away from her. But Leopard leaped forward and grabbed Baboon by the throat. "You let that tasty, fat Dassie escape," Leopard scolded. "Perhaps I should eat you instead!" And she opened her mouth to take a bite.

"Wait!" squealed Baboon. "Let me pay you for my mistake!"

"How?" Leopard snarled.

"By revealing a secret to you," said Baboon. "This is not the way to kill a baboon. You must drop a baboon from a great height so that it shatters into many bite-sized pieces. We are much tastier that way."

Leopard was astounded.

"Throw me up into the air by this tree," chattered Baboon, "and I will fall and break into a hundred tender little pieces."

Leopard was very hungry, but she couldn't resist the idea of eating Baboon as tender morsels, so she tossed Baboon high into the air. In a flash, Baboon reached out and grabbed a tree branch. Then he screamed that she was ugly before swinging through the highest tree branches until he was far out of sight.

Leopard never forgot the embarrassment of being so foolish, and she never forgave Baboon for calling her ugly. To this day, leopards kill and eat baboons whenever they can catch one. And baboons scream insults at leopards—from a safe distance.

GLOSSARY

adaptable – having the ability to change to improve one's chances of survival in an environment

camouflage – the ability to hide, due to coloring or markings that blend in with a given environment

captive-rearing – raising offspring in a place from which escape is not possible

carcass – the dead body of an animal

coat of arms – the official symbol of a family, state, nation, or other group

ethnic – sharing distinctive cultural traits as a group in society

evolve – to gradually develop into a new form

excavated – revealed or removed from the ground by digging earth from an area

extinct – having no living members

food chains – systems in nature in which living things are dependent on each other for food

genetic – relating to genes, the basic physical units of heredity

land bridge – a piece of land connecting two landmasses that allowed people and animals to pass from one place to another

mortality rate – the number of deaths in a certain area or period

mosaics – pictures or designs made by arranging small pieces of colored material such as glass, stone, or tile

mythology – a collection of myths, or popular, traditional beliefs or stories that explain how something came to be or that are associated with a person or object

pelts – the skins of animals with the fur or wool still attached

poaching – hunting protected species of wild animals, even though doing so is against the law

radio collars – collars fitted with small electronic devices that send signals to radio receivers

retina – a layer or lining in the back of the eye that is sensitive to light

retractable – able to be drawn in from an extended position

semidesert – a partly dry area located between a desert and a grassland or forest

shrine – a place associated with a holy person or thing

SELECTED BIBLIOGRAPHY

Bailey, Theodore N. *The African Leopard: Ecology and Behavior of a Solitary Felid.* Caldwell, N.J.: Blackburn Press, 2005.

Defenders of Wildlife. "Leopard." Kids' Planet. http://www.kidsplanet.org/factsheets/leopard.html.

Gamble, Cyndi. *Leopards.* St. Paul: Voyageur Press, 2004.

Kure, Nils. *Living with Leopards.* Cape Town, South Africa: Sunbird, 2003.

National Geographic. "Leopard." Animals. http://animals.nationalgeographic.com/animals/mammals/leopard.html.

Singh, Arian. *Prince of Cats.* New York: Oxford University Press, 2001.

Leopards are most comfortable moving about at dawn and dusk, and they rarely hunt in the full light of day.

INDEX